Cuts, Scrapes, Scabs, *and* Scars

Dr. Alvin Silverstein,

Virginia Silverstein, and

Laura Silverstein Nunn

My Health
Franklin Watts

A Division of Grolier Publishing

New York • London • Hong Kong • Sydney

Danbury, Connecticut

Your Healing Body

Ouch! That hurts! You just fell off your bike again and scraped your knee. It probably wasn't the first time this happened, and it surely will not be the last. When kids are active, accidents are bound to happen. The truth is, you will get plenty of cuts, scratches, **scrapes,** and bruises during your lifetime.

Fortunately, people have amazing bodies. The "boo-boos" you get usually go away in almost no time at all because your body has special ways to heal damaged skin. Let's find out what happens when we get hurt and how our bodies heal.

Did You Know...

Kids heal much faster than adults.

◀ **Another scraped knee—part of a typical day's play.**

Your Amazing Skin

All animals have skin. It acts as a protective covering for the body. Skin can serve a variety of purposes. Some animals have skin that acts like a suit of armor, helping to protect them from enemies. And some animals have skin with the same color as their environment, making it hard for enemies to spot them.

A porcupine's skin is covered with sharp, prickly spines called quills. If an enemy tries to bite a porcupine, it will get a mouthful of quills. A chameleon

A porcupine's spiny quills help to protect it.

A chameleon's skin changes color, helping it to blend into its surroundings.

can change the color of its skin to blend with its sur-roundings. Its skin helps to hide it from enemies and catch smaller animals—it can sneak up on an insect without being noticed.

Your skin is not covered with prickly spines, and it cannot change color to match your surroundings, but it protects you all the same. It acts like a waterproof overcoat that protects your body from injury and disease. What's more, it is a coat that never wears out because it can mend itself when it gets torn!

Your skin is made up of billions of tiny cells—cells so small you need a microscope to see them. You probably think that all your skin cells are alive. That would seem to make sense. After all, as you grow,

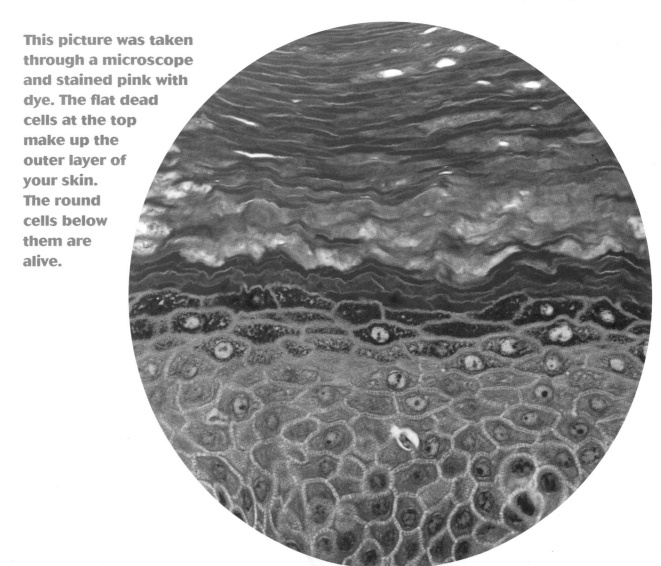

This picture was taken through a microscope and stained pink with dye. The flat dead cells at the top make up the outer layer of your skin. The round cells below them are alive.

your skin grows with you. But actually, some of the cells in your skin are dead. The average skin cell lives just 28 days, and new cells are constantly forming inside your skin.

As new cells form, they push the dead ones up toward the outside of the body. The dead cells are squeezed together and flattened to form a thick, tough outer layer. These dead cells are mostly made of a **pro-tein** called *keratin*. Some of the dead cells in this outer keratin layer flake off whenever you touch something.

The keratin layer is an important form of protection. The cells on the skin's surface overlap one another like the shingles on a roof. Just as a roof keeps the rain out of your house, the keratin layer keeps most disease germs from getting through your skin. If the germs can't get in, they can't hurt you. The cells that make up your thick keratin layer also keep body fluids from leaking out.

A Huge Loss

When you shake someone's hand or wash your hands, you may lose as many as 40,000 dead skin cells in 1 minute!

Just beneath the keratin layer, there are two layers of living skin cells. The top layer is called the **epidermis**. The epidermis is about as thick as a sheet of paper—much thinner than the keratin layer. When cells in the epidermis layer die, they move up into the keratin layer.

Below the epidermis is another layer of living skin cells called the **dermis**. The dermis makes up about 90 percent of the skin. The dermis has **glands** that give off sweat when you are hot and produce oils when your skin is dry. Your hair grows out of **hair follicles** in the dermis. The dermis also contains many muscles and nerve endings. The nerves tell you when things are

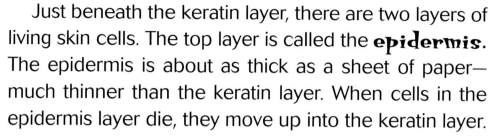

This picture shows skin from the palm of a hand. Can you identify the keratin layer? Do you see the dermis and epidermis?

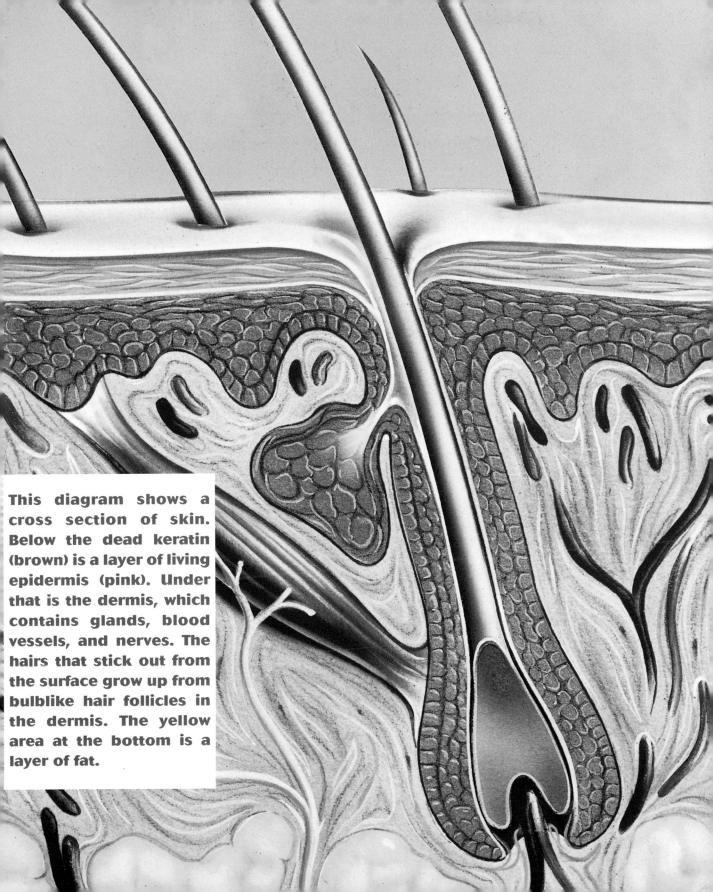

This diagram shows a cross section of skin. Below the dead keratin (brown) is a layer of living epidermis (pink). Under that is the dermis, which contains glands, blood vessels, and nerves. The hairs that stick out from the surface grow up from bulblike hair follicles in the dermis. The yellow area at the bottom is a layer of fat.

hot or cold, or when something is hurting you. For instance, when you cut your finger, nerve endings in the dermis send messages to your brain that your finger is hurt.

The living cells in the dermis are nourished by millions of tiny blood vessels, called **capillaries**. The epidermis has no blood vessels. That's why slight scratches don't bleed. The cells in the epidermis depend on the blood vessels in the dermis for the food and oxygen they need to live and grow.

When the Skin Is Broken

You can hurt yourself anytime, anywhere. You can get a paper cut on your lip or tongue when you are licking an envelope to seal it. You can get scratches on your hands when you play with a cat. Or you can get scratches on your legs when you walk through a field where blackberry bushes grow.

Cats are fun to play with, but they have sharp claws that can scratch your skin.

When something hard or sharp hits your body, the first thing to get hurt is your skin. When you get a cut, chemicals inside your skin cells leak out, and your pain nerves carry a message to the brain.

The deeper or wider a cut, the greater the pain. Larger cuts mean that more cells are damaged. More chemicals spill out of the cells into the tissues, so more pain messages travel to the brain. As a result, you feel more pain.

What Paper, Oranges, and Salt Have in Common

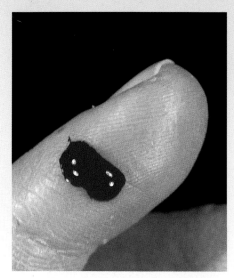

Even a small cut on a finger can bleed and hurt.

Have you ever had a paper cut that hurt *really* badly? Most paper cuts are very minor injuries, so why do they hurt so much? Because it is not the cut that is actually causing the pain. It is the chemicals in the paper reacting with the nerves in your skin.

Have you ever eaten an orange when you had a cut on your hand? If the juice got into the cut, that probably hurt too. The acid in the juice made your cut sting. The salt in ocean water can also make a cut sting.

Activity 1: Kinds of Wounds

With a nail file or an emery board, gently rub the surface of an apple. Rub it until there is a spot on the skin that is rough and dull looking. You have made a wound on the apple, like the scrape you get when you fall and "skin your knee." Only the outer surface is rubbed off. The wound does not go all the way through the apple's skin, just as a scrape on your knee may not go below the epidermis.

Next, rub on a different spot. This time, rub until you break through the apple's red skin and get down to the juicy, white pulp. This scrape is deeper. Juice seeps out of the wound on the apple, like blood seeps out of a bad scrape on your skin.

Now carefully cut a small wedge out of the apple. Knives can be dangerous, so ask an adult to help you. You should see lots of juice seeping out. The knife has done the same type of damage to the apple that it could do to your finger.

After a few hours, look at the wounds on the apple again. The cut surfaces have dried out and turned brown. That's the apple's way of limiting the damage to as small an area as possible. But an apple cannot heal its wounds the way your body can!

As soon as you hurt yourself, your body goes into action. When tiny blood cells called **platelets** come across a damaged blood vessel, they become sticky. They catch on the rough edges of the cut and stick to the injured blood vessel. As more and more platelets arrive at the scene, they pile up. Eventually, they form a plug that fills the hole and stops the bleeding. Without platelets, you could bleed to death from just a small cut.

These plate-lets help blood to clot and stop the bleeding from a cut.

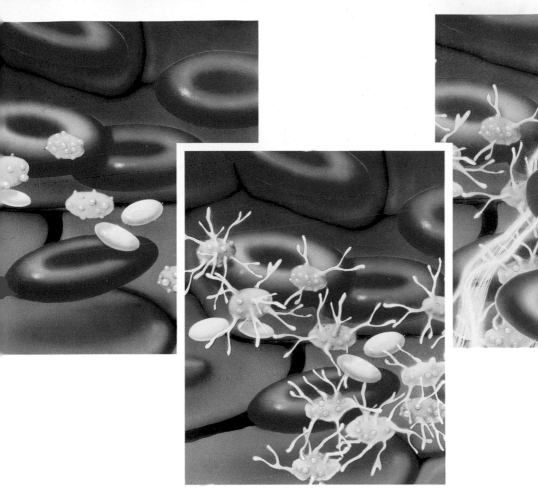

When an injury occurs, platelets (yellow) gather in the damaged tissues and break open (left), forming a protein called fibrin (center). Strands of fibrin form a tangled mesh that traps red blood cells (red) to produce a jellylike clot (right).

Platelets are so delicate that some break open when they touch the rough edges of a cut. The materials that spill out of the broken platelets produce a protein called **fibrin**. Strands of fibrin form a mesh over the injured area, trapping **red blood cells** in the web. This makes the blood start to thicken. Eventually, it turns into a jellylike substance called a **clot**. When the blood dries, this blood clot forms a hard **scab** over the wound.

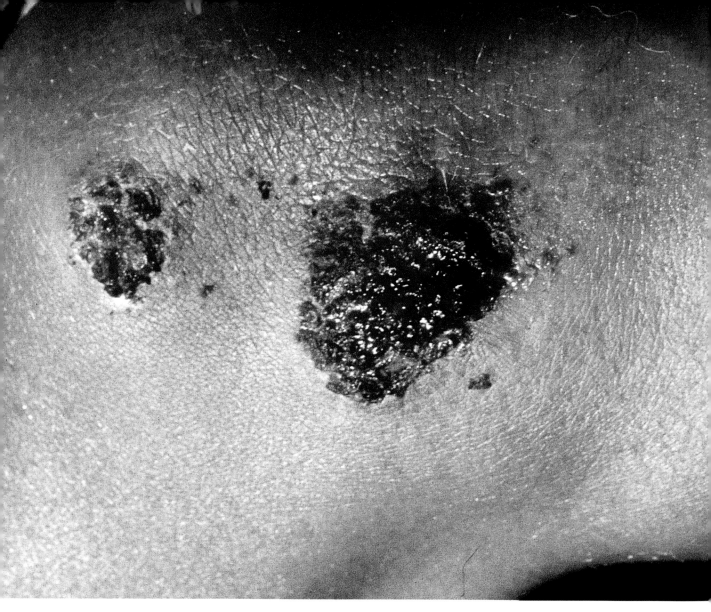

The blood clot that formed over this scraped elbow has dried into a hard scab that will protect the delicate tissues underneath until the skin has healed.

Scabs are a very important part of the healing process. They protect cuts from more damage. If you pick at a scab, it may take longer for your cut to heal.

The Fix-Up Job

Underneath the scab, the wound starts to heal. You may not realize it, but while you are playing outside or eating lunch, there's a lot of activity going on inside your cut. First, your body cleans out the wound, then it repairs the damage.

Undercover Wounds

If you fall and bump your elbow, you may not get a cut that breaks the skin. But that doesn't mean your body hasn't been damaged. If your elbow is sore or swollen and turns kind of purple in a day or so, you have a **bruise.**

Even though you can't see any damage, the tissue inside has been torn and blood is leaking out of tiny broken blood vessels. The purple color is blood seen through layers of skin. When the blood cells start to break down, the bruise gradually becomes yellow or green. Eventually, the bruise fades away.

Soccer players get lots of bumps and bruises, like the one on this girl's thigh.

After a fall off a bike, the tissues in this scraped knee are getting swollen and inflamed.

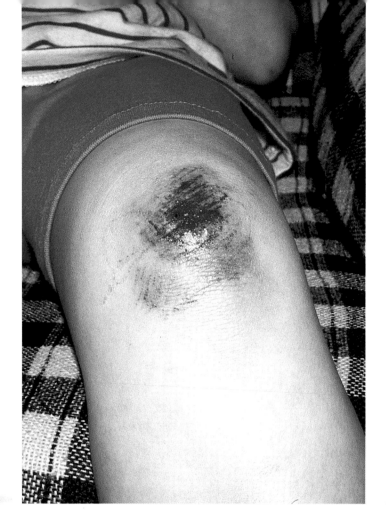

Damaged cells send out chemicals that tell the body that something is wrong. Some of these materials cause leaks in the walls of the tiny blood vessels in the skin. Fluid from the blood seeps out into the tissues, which then become swollen. This is part of a body reaction called **inflammation**. If this medical word sounds a bit like "flame," that is not surprising. Inflamed tissues are not only swollen, they are often hot and red, as though there were a fire inside them.

The damaged blood vessels also release materials that send signals. They call in the clean-up squad—the **white blood cells**. White blood cells are jellylike blobs that can change their shape. Unlike the other cells in your body, the white blood cells can swim. They move by pushing out a bulge from their body. The rest of the jelly flows into the bulge, and the cell moves along.

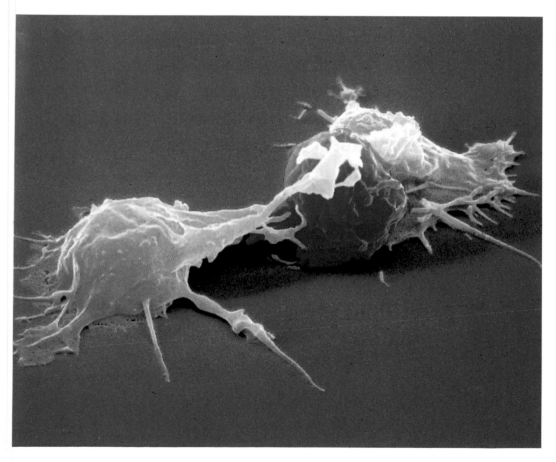

These white blood cells are attacking a cell that has invaded the body.

The Battle with Bacteria

Normally, your skin protects you from outside invaders. But when your skin is cut open, dirt and germs can get inside your body—and that can mean trouble. In some cases, invading **bacteria** can **infect** the tissues around the cut. When this happens, the area becomes red, swollen, and very sore.

When your body senses invaders, chemical alarm signals call for help. White blood cells come to fight the bacteria. When they arrive, a serious battle takes place. The white blood cells swarm over the bacteria and eat them. During the battle, some white blood cells are killed by the bacteria. The dead bodies of the white cells pile up to form **pus.** The body keeps sending more and more white blood cells into battle until they kill off all the bacteria. Your skin will stay red and swollen until the fight is over.

Eating the Enemy

White blood cells destroy bacteria and other invaders in much the same way that you eat food. White blood cells break down invaders with digestive juices very similar to the ones in your stomach.

28

If an infection gets really bad, bacteria can spread to other parts of your body. This could make you very sick. If your infected cut does not look better in 2 or 3 days, have it checked by a doctor. You may need an antibiotic to help bring the infection under control.

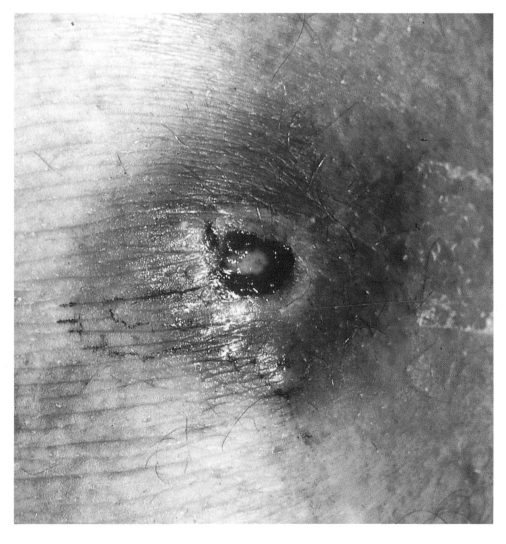

A thorn that carried bacteria into the skin produced this infected wound. The white material in the center is pus.

Treating a Cut

Most cuts are fairly easy to treat. The first thing you should do is wash the cut thoroughly with soap and water. You need to use an antiseptic to kill any bacteria in the wound. Then put some antibacterial ointment on the cut to help the healing process. The wound should also be covered with a bandage or Band-Aid® to protect it until a scab forms. Once the wound has crusted over with a scab, your body will take care of the rest.

Prompt first aid can help a wound to heal better.

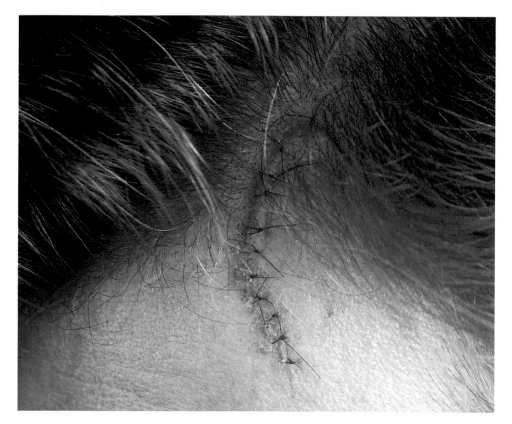

This bad cut on the forehead was closed with stitches.

If a cut is very large or deep, you may need stitches. If the bleeding just won't stop, it's time for a trip to the hospital. Getting stitches for a cut is kind of like sewing a rip in a shirt. A doctor uses a very clean needle and thread to sew the two edges of the wound together. Stitches help stop the bleeding, and they also keep the wound from becoming infected. Within about a week or so, the wound heals and the doctor can take the stitches out.

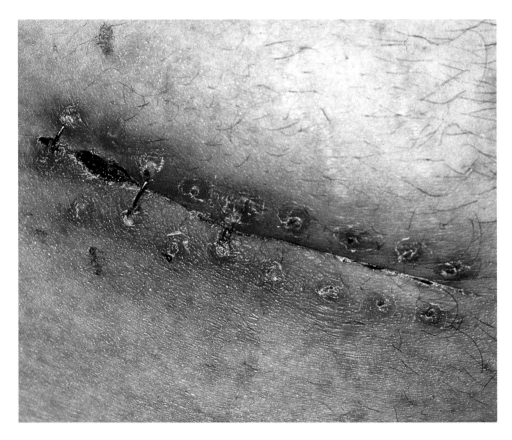

Surgeon's removed this person's appendix and closed the wound with staples. But the patient did not keep the wound clean enough, and it got infected. Now it must be treated with antibiotics.

Instead of stitches, doctors may close a wound with staples or with little strips of tape called butterflies because they look like butterfly wings. Sometimes doctors use medical glue. Medical glue is a special glue that has been changed and sterilized for medical purposes. Studies have shown that closing a wound with medical glue is less painful than stitches, and the wound heals just as well. Unfortunately, it cannot be used on the feet, hands, or joints.

Activity 2: Let's Play Doctor!

Do you have an old stuffed toy that is pretty banged up? Maybe there are some cuts or tears in its "skin" that need to be fixed. If you were an Emergency Room doctor and the toy were your patient, what would you do? Should you use a needle and thread to stitch up the cut? Or would it be better to use a stapler, a strip of surgical tape, or glue to repair the wound? Try all these methods and see which ones work best.

OUCH!

Have you ever stepped on a thumbtack or had a small piece of wood stuck in your finger? Even though only a small section of skin was broken, these **punc-ture wounds** may be quite deep. If the thumbtack or wood was dirty, some of the dirt may stay inside the wound when the object is pulled out. Bacteria on the object might also be left behind.

Or, even worse, part of the piece of wood might break off and get stuck inside you. Now you have a **splinter**. If the splinter is sticking out of the skin, use tweezers to try to get it out. For splinters that are tough to get out, try soaking your skin—this helps loosen the skin and makes the job easier. As a last

Hidden Dangers

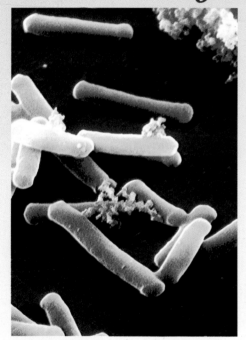

These are tetanus bacteria, shown 10,000 times their real size.

Have you ever stepped on a rusty nail? Rusty nails are sometimes covered with **tetanus** bacteria. These bacteria don't cause too much trouble in shallow wounds, but they multiply quickly inside deep wounds, such as puncture wounds.

If these bacteria spread into your bloodstream, they can cause a condition called "lockjaw." Your muscles get so stiff that you can't move. You can't even open your mouth to eat or talk. Tetanus bacteria can even cause death. Babies are given shots to protect them against tetanus, but the protection doesn't last forever. You should get a "booster shot" every 10 years to stay protected.

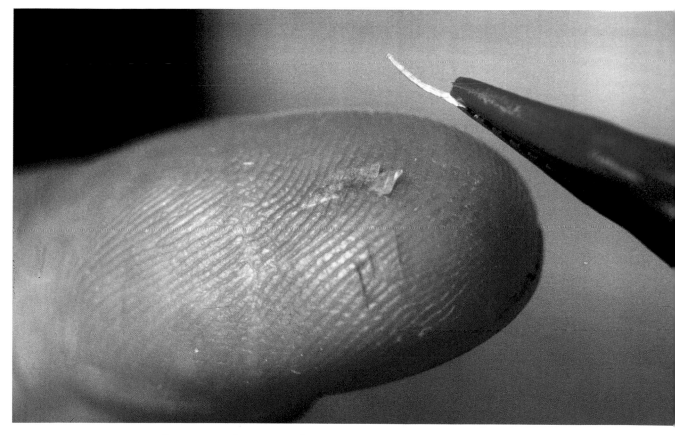

Tweezers can help in removing a splinter.

resort, have an adult use a needle cleaned with alcohol to try to pick the out splinter. But always be gentle. After you get the splinter out, wash the wounded area and put antibacterial ointment on it.

If a splinter is left in the skin, it can be very painful for days, and may possibly cause an infection. If there are any signs of problems, go to the doctor.

Eating healthful foods will also help your body heal faster.

usually eat? Do you eat plenty of fruits and vegetables, or do you eat a lot junk food? What you eat has a very important effect on how you feel and how you heal.

Some vitamins help in wound healing. One of the best known is vitamin A. Vitamin A keeps your skin strong. Without vitamin A, the layers of your skin become weakened, making it easier for you to injure your skin. Vitamin C is another important healing vitamin. Vitamin C helps to keep your body strong, which also helps the healing process. Vitamin E helps your body heal too. Without vitamin E, your body cannot make enough collagen to help wounds heal. A mineral called selenium helps vitamin E to work. You can remember the important nutrients for healthy healing by thinking of the word "ACES."

Take good care of your body, and it will help take care of you.

Foods that Help You Heal

Vitamin A	Vitamin C	Vitamin E	Selenium
Broccoli	Cantaloupe	Margarine	Beef
Carrots	Grapefruit	Olives	Chicken
Eggs	Grapefruit juice	Vegetable oil	Eggs
Kale	Green peppers	Wheat germ	Fish
Liver	Kiwi	Whole grains	Garlic
Milk	Lemonade		Liver
Mustard greens	Lemons		Shellfish
Sweet potatoes	Limes		Wheat germ
Yellow squash	Oranges		Whole grains
Zucchini	Orange juice		
	Tomatoes		
	Tomato juice		

Index

Page numbers in *italics* indicate illustrations.

About the Authors

Dr. Alvin Silverstein is a Professor of Biology at the College of Staten Island of the City University of New York. **Virginia Silverstein** is a translator of Russian scientific literature. The Silversteins first worked together on a research project at the University of Pennsylvania. Since then, they have produced six children and more than 150 published books for young people.

Laura Silverstein Nunn, a graduate of Kean College, has been helping with her parents' books since her high school days. She is the coauthor of more than twenty books on diseases and health, science concepts, endangered species, and pets. Laura lives with her husband Matt and their young son Cory in a rural New Jersey town not far from her childhood home.